SMALL ECO-HOUSES
PETITES MAISONS ÉCOLOGIQUES
KLEINE ÖKOHÄUSER

SMALL ECO-HOUSES
PETITES MAISONS ÉCOLOGIQUES
KLEINE ÖKOHÄUSER

EVERGREEN

EVERGREEN is an imprint of

TASCHEN GmbH

© 2007 TASCHEN GmbH

Hohenzollernring 53, D-50672 Köln

www.taschen.com

Editor Editrice Redakteur:
Simone Schleifer

English translation Traduction anglaise Englische Übersetzung:
Julia Hendler, Gene Ferber

French translation Traduction française Französische Übersetzung:
Marion Westerhoff

German translation Traduction allemande Deutsche Übersetzung:
Susanne Engler

Proofreading Relecture Korrektur lesen:
Ian Ayers, Catherine Collins

Art director Direction artistique Art Direktor:
Mireia Casanovas Soley

Graphic design and layout Mise en page et maquette Graphische Gestaltung und Layout:
Laura Millán

Printed by Imprimé par Gedruckt durch:
Gráficas Toledo, Spain

ISBN 978-3-8228-4049-8

"Building means destroying the environment!" – this is a reproach that many architects often hear throughout their careers. And actually, the inconsiderate treatment of the environment and out-of-date techniques that have been used in construction have contributed greatly towards generating this image: it deals with buildings that are erected as a burden from the moment that construction starts and that, consequently, are a dead weight for its inhabitant, the environment, and following generations. At the same time, one's house, this place created by humans for millennia, is the most important of our vital spaces. In it we feel alive and, as well, we hope to capture our esthetic visions, in order to be able to transmit them as a legacy to our children.

A house is, for all these reasons, more than a place. It is a fragment of "constructive responsibility" because it should not only protect its guests but also be respectful of the environment and considerate of the resources of humanity. In this sense, we pose the question of if –in our current world– there is the possibility of creating a certain balance between the impacts that architecture generates and the maintenance of an intact environment. The possibility of carrying this out exists. But what is feasible technically speaking, in the majority of the cases, is more difficult to apply in reality. The person, when building, who looks for that balance point and wishes to construct truly ecological houses, should make an effort, often during many years, to make comprehensible that which is, by any reckoning, logical. Fortunately, the emergence of a stronger awareness in regards to the environment, the introduction of more and new technical knowledge, and the application of traditional construction methods, such as the orientation towards the sun, is bringing a growing number of owners to build ecological houses on a small scale. These small eco-houses constitute a first step towards a culture of sustainable and responsible construction. This is not based only on using natural materials, that save energy and contain environmental contamination, but in building small oasises that offer their tenants a high quality of life. There are numerous examples that show how pleasant ecological houses can be from an architectural point of view, independent of the material used in construction, whether it be stone, wood, or brick. The great variety of ecologic materials available allows architects to choose their own approach.

What makes an ecological house particular? Essentially it is, without a doubt, the use of renewable energies as well as the use of different methods to save energy. The great majority of eco-houses are equipped with hot water collectors, photovoltaic installations, accumulators, biomass boilers and reduced electrical usage. From pioneers in the construction of eco-houses, we have learned building standards that are respectful of the environment. These are homes that are practically energy self-sufficient or "passive" houses. The self-sufficient houses that, like small power stations, produce more energy than their tenants require, constitute the culminating point of this development. For their construction they also use primarily natural and recyclable materials and apply, likewise, indigenous construction materials to promote regional development and the establishment of new means of transportation.

This book presents a selection of small eco-houses, built according to what is today feasible in the field of the architecture. Considered as architectural curiosities for some time, these houses, built in a manner this is respectful to the environment, lay the foundation for tomorrow's construction. And, they invite us to propose that we can not just pursue our own quality of life, but that we should leave a future for our children and grandchildren in which they can feel at home, and where feeling comfortable in an dignified environment is a truism.

Rolf Disch

« Construire c'est détruire l'environnement! » –C'est un reproche que beaucoup d'architectes ne cessent de s'entendre répéter tout au long de leur vie professionnelle. Il est vrai qu'une approche inconsidérée de l'environnement et des normes de construction surannées ont contribué à nourrir cette image négative : des édifices qui, dès leur construction, sont une charge et source de pollution, deviennent ainsi un fardeau pour les habitants, l'environnement et les générations futures. Et pourtant, la maison, cet espace créé par les hommes durant des siècles, est notre univers le plus cher : l'endroit où l'on se sent bien et en sécurité. Par ailleurs, nous voulons aussi que ces constructions reflètent nos concepts esthétiques, pour pouvoir les transmettre et en léguer la valeur à nos enfants.

Mais une maison, c'est bien plus que cela : c'est une forme « de responsabilité construite ». Il ne s'agit pas uniquement de protéger ses habitants, mais, également de traiter l'environnement et les ressources humaines à bon escient. Et l'on vient alors à se demander si, dans notre monde moderne, il est possible d'instaurer un équilibre entre l'impact généré par l'architecture et la préservation d'un environnement intact. Nous avons certainement les moyens de le faire. Mais justement ce qui est réalisable sur le plan technique, est en réalité souvent plus difficile à concrétiser. Qui veut sortir des normes habituelles et construire une maison vraiment écologique doit souvent déployer une énergie considérable, sur plusieurs années, pour finalement réaliser et faire admettre ce qui semble tout à fait normal. Fort heureusement, une prise de conscience accrue de l'environnement, les découvertes techniques récentes, ainsi que le retour aux méthodes de construction traditionnelles, comme l'orientation en fonction du soleil, conduisent nombre de maîtres d'ouvrage à construire des maisons écologiques de petite taille. Ce type d'habitation est le premier pas vers une politique architecturale plus durable et responsable. D'ailleurs, il ne s'agit pas uniquement d'utiliser des matériaux de construction plus naturels, de réduire de manière exemplaire la consommation d'énergie et d'éviter les substances polluantes. Il s'agit surtout de créer des petites oasis génératrices d'une qualité de vie supérieure au profit de ses habitants. Une foule d'exemples montre le charme architectural des maisons écologiques, qu'elles soient réalisées en pierre, bois ou torchis. La vaste panoplie de matériaux écologiques permet aux architectes d'envisager des solutions individuelles pour chaque projet.

Que caractérise une maison écologique? C'est essentiellement l'emploi d'énergies renouvelables et de diverses méthodes pour réduire la consommation d'énergie. La plupart des maisons écologiques sont équipées de capteurs tubulaires d'eau chaude, installations à cellules photovoltaïques, échangeurs de chaleur, fours à biomasse ou de petits groupes électrogènes. C'est ainsi que les pionniers dans la construction de maisons écologiques ont jeté les bases des normes environnementales actuelles : les maisons à fonctionnement passif et à faible énergie. Les derniers modèles de « maisons énergie plus » –à plus haut rendement énergétique– qui, à l'instar de petites centrales électriques produisent plus d'énergie que nécessaire à ses habitants, sont l'apogée de ce développement. Ces maisons sont construites essentiellement à partir de matériaux naturels et recyclables, provenant, en outre, du marché local pour encourager le développement écologique régional tout en réduisant les transports inutiles.

Cet ouvrage illustre, grâce aux petites maisons écologiques sélectionnées ici, ce qui est réalisable en domaine de construction durable. Il propose des alternatives architecturales concrètes. Longtemps considérées comme curiosités architecturales, les maisons écologiques respectueuses de l'environnement posent les normes de la construction de demain. Grâce à elles, nous pouvons déjà nous octroyer une certaine qualité de vie, mais nous pouvons surtout offrir à nos enfants et petits-enfants un avenir où il sera tout à fait naturel de se sentir chez soi et se sentir bien dans un environnement digne d'être vécu.

Rolf Disch

„Bauen ist Umweltzerstörung!" – diesen Vorwurf müssen sich viele Architekten im Laufe ihres Lebens immer wieder anhören. Und tatsächlich haben der unsensible Umgang mit der Umwelt und überholte Baustandards vielfach zu einem solchen Bild beigetragen: Gebäude, die bereits während ihrer Entstehung zu Altlasten anwachsen und die für die Bewohner, die Umwelt und künftige Generationen zur Bürde werden. Dabei ist das Haus, dieser seit Jahrtausenden vom Menschen geschaffene Raum, unser wichtigster Lebensraum. Hier fühlen wir uns geborgen. Zugleich wollen wir in der Gestaltung der Bauwerke unseren ästhetischen Ansprüchen gerecht werden, um sie damit als wertvolles Gut an unsere Kinder weitergeben zu können.

Doch ein Haus ist noch mehr: Es ist ein Stück „gebaute Verantwortung". Es muss nicht nur seine Bewohner schützen, sondern auch mit der Umwelt und den Ressourcen der Menschheit sorgsam umgehen. Es stellt sich die Frage, ob in unserer modernen Welt eine Balance zwischen den Eingriffen der Architektur und einer intakten Umwelt entstehen kann. Die Möglichkeiten sind vorhanden. Aber gerade was technisch im Bereich des Machbaren liegt, ist in der Realität meist nur schwer zu erreichen. Wer beim Bauen über das gängige Mittelmaß hinausgehen und wirklich ökologische Häuser bauen will, muss oft jahrelang großen Einsatz aufbringen, um das eigentlich Selbstverständliche wahr zu machen. Glücklicherweise veranlassen das erstarkte Umweltbewusstsein, neueste wissenschaftliche Erkenntnisse, sowie die Rückbesinnung auf traditionelle Baumethoden, wie beispielsweise die Ausrichtung nach der Sonne, mehr und mehr Bauherren dazu, ökologische Häuser im kleinen Maßstab zu errichten. Solche kleinen Ökohäuser sind der erste Schritt in die Richtung einer nachhaltigen und verantwortungsvollen Baukultur. Dabei geht es nicht nur darum, natürliche Baustoffe zu verwenden, beispielhaft Energien einzusparen und Schadstoffe zu vermeiden. Es geht darum, kleine Oasen zu schaffen, die ihren Bewohnern Lebensqualität auf höchstem Niveau bieten. Es gibt zahlreiche Beispiele, die zeigen, wie architektonisch anmutig ökologische Häuser sein können, egal ob es sich dabei um Stein-, Holz- oder Lehmhäuser handelt. Die große Vielfalt an ökologischen Materialien erlaubt jedem Architekten individuelle Lösungsansätze.

Was macht ökologische Häuser eigentlich aus? Das Wesentliche dabei ist der Einsatz regenerativer Energien und verschiedenster Energie-Einsparmethoden. Die meisten der Ökohäuser sind mit Warmwasser-Röhrenkollektoren, Photovoltaikanlagen, Wärmetauschern, Biomasse-Öfen oder kleinen Blockheizkraftwerken ausgestattet. Damit wurden von den Bau-Pionieren der ökologischen Häuser die heute gängigen Umweltstandards geschaffen: die Niedrigenergie- und Passivhäuser. Modernste Plusenergiehäuser, die als kleine Kraftwerke mehr Energie produzieren, als ihre Bewohner benötigen, sind der Höhepunkt dieser Entwicklung. Es werden vorwiegend natürliche und recyclebare Materialien zur Errichtung der Häuser verwendet. Zugleich werden lokale Baustoffe eingesetzt und dadurch regionale ökologische Entwicklungen gefördert und weite Transportwege vermieden.

Das vorliegende Buch illustriert anhand ausgewählter kleiner ökologischer Häuser, was im Bereich nachhaltigen Bauens machbar ist. Es zeigt die konkreten Alternativen, die sich in der Architektur bieten. Lange als Kuriosum der Baukunst betrachtet, setzen umweltverträglich gebaute Häuser die Standards für das Bauen von morgen. Sie zeigen, dass wir damit nicht nur uns selbst Lebensqualität bescheren, sondern auch unseren Kindern und Enkelkindern eine Zukunft schenken können, in der Sich-Zuhausefühlen und Sich-Wohlfühlen in einer lebenswerten Umwelt eine Selbstverständlichkeit sind.

Rolf Disch

Rolf Disch

> Homes that produce more energy than needed by its inhabitants
> Improve the quality of life by using sustainable construction materials
> Solar power as the primary source of energy

> Maisons produisant plus d'énergie que nécessaire
> Meilleure qualité de vie grâce à des matériaux sains
> Energie solaire comme moteur de la société

> Häuser, die mehr Energie produzieren, als ihre Bewohner verbrauchen können
> Hohe Lebensqualität mit gesunden Baustoffen
> Sonnenenergie als Motor der Gesellschaft

His architecture maintains the relation between functionality, ecology and design while it is considered vanguard by the professional community.

The need to change this vision from a utopian dream into an everyday reality is the starting premise for all of the architectural work of Disch and his team.

In acknowledgement for this innovative work, Rolf Disch's architectural firm has received numerous prizes and much recognition over the years including the European Solar Energy Prize in 2002 and one year later the World Energy Globe.

Son architecture conjugue fonction, écologie et esthétique. Les experts en la matière qualifient ses projets de futuristes.

Cette vision ne doit certes pas demeurer une utopie. L'architecte et son équipe nous en fournissent la preuve visuelle par le biais d'une foule de projets les plus divers.

Le travail du bureau d'architecture a été récompensé par de nombreux prix et distinctions.

En 2002, Rolf Disch reçoit, entre autres, le Prix Solaire Européen et un an plus tard, se voit décerner la distinction du World Energy Globe.

Seine Architektur steht für die Verbindung von Funktion, Ökologie und Ästhetik und seine Projekte werden von der Fachwelt als zukunftsweisend angesehen.

Dass diese Vision keine Utopie bleiben muss, haben er und sein Team bewiesen und die Vielzahl unterschiedlichster Bauprojekte bezeugt dies anschaulich.

Das Architekturbüro wurde für seine innovative Arbeit mit zahlreichen Preisen und Auszeichnungen honoriert; so erhielt Rolf Disch unter anderem 2002 den Europäischen Solarpreis und wurde ein Jahr später mit dem World Energy Globe ausgezeichnet.

SMALL ECO-HOUSES
PETITES MAISONS ÉCOLOGIQUES
KLEINE ÖKOHÄUSER

☐ Lavaflow 2

Craig Steely

This house rises above the coast at the only stretch of black sand that there is on this side of the island. The home is built on a cantilevered concrete platform that elevates it 180 cm, so that minimizes its footprint on the land and avoids contact with the surrounding lava. In the subfloor space there is a tank that collects rain water. Thanks to the concrete walls, the water remains cool and in the shade so that it also avoids chlorine treatments for its disinfection. The walls of the home combine glass and wood. The sliding doors take advantage of the breeze as a natural cooling system. The structure and the lines of the home frame the landscape: the lava, sea and sky. This building offers an example of how architecture and landscape can coexist in a sustainable and ecological manner.

Cette maison s'érige face à la côte, sur l'unique espace de sable noir présent de ce côté de l'île. L'habitation est située sur une plateforme de béton en porte-à-faux qui surélève le rez-de-chaussée de 180 cm, minimisant ainsi la surface d'appui sur le terrain et évitant le contact avec la lave des alentours. Cet espace accueille une citerne qui recueille les eaux de pluie. Grâce aux murs de béton, l'eau reste à l'ombre et fraîche, évitant ainsi un traitement au chlore pour la désinfecter. Les murs de l'habitation conjuguent verre et bois. Les portes coulissantes créent un système de circulation d'air utilisé comme système de climatisation naturelle. La structure et les lignes de l'habitation encadrent le paysage : la lave, la mer et le ciel. Cette construction est un exemple de cohabitation possible, durable et écologique, entre l'architecture et le paysage.

Dieses Haus erhebt sich direkt an der Küste auf einem einzigartigen Gelände mit schwarzem Sand, den es auf dieser Seite der Insel gibt. Das Haus steht auf einer überstehenden Betonplattform, die es 180 cm vom Boden abhebt. So ist die Fläche, die sich direkt auf den Boden stützt, sehr klein, und man vermeidet den Kontakt mit der Lava der Umgebung. Der dadurch entstandene Raum wird für eine Regenwasserzisterne genutzt. Aufgrund der Betonwände bleibt das Wasser im Schatten und somit kühl, und muss nicht mit Chlor desinfiziert werden. An den Wänden des Hauses wurde Glas mit Holz kombiniert. Die Schiebetüren machen es möglich, den Wind und Luftströme als natürliches Kühlsystem zu benutzen. Die Struktur und die Linien des Gebäudes umrahmen die Landschaft: die Lava, das Meer und den Himmel. Es handelt sich um ein Beispiel dafür, wie man Architektur und Landschaft auf sanfte und ökologische Weise miteinander kombinieren kann.

The unique landscape of volcanic rock around the house creates an impression of aridity complimented by the surrounding vegetation and the nearby ocean.

Dû à ses roches de lave, le paysage unique qui entoure la maison donne une certaine impression d'aridité, compensée cependant par la végétation environnante et l'océan proche.

Die einzigartige Landschaft, die das Haus umgibt, wirkt durch das Lavagestein einerseits karg, wird jedoch durch die Pflanzen und den nahen Ozean kontrastiert.

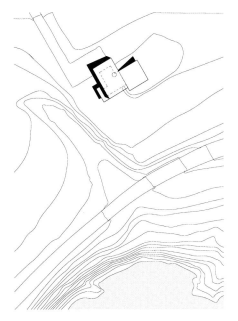

Site plan Plan de situation Umgebungsplan

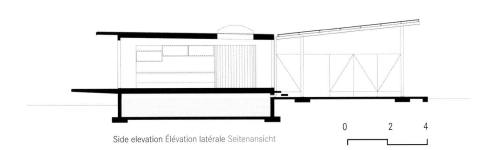

Side elevation Élévation latérale Seitenansicht

0   2   4

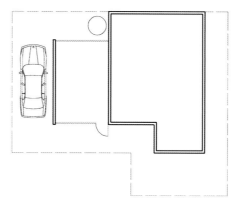

Lower level Niveau inférieur Untere Ebene

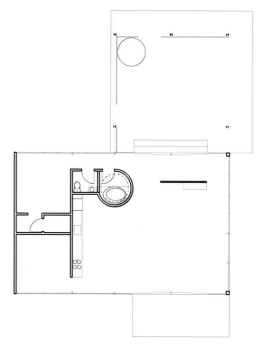

Upper level Niveau supérieur Obere Ebene

0   1   2

☐ Solar House I
Maison Solaire I
Solarhaus I

GLASSX AG, Dietrich Schwarz

Solar House I is a zero-energy house built in the depression of the Rhein, parallel to the valley. The opaque photovoltaic panels on the eastern, western and southern façades are separated by windows reaching floor level. Given the low energy contribution from the north, no collectors are needed on that side and the whole northern façade consists of a large panoramic window. The shell of the building is made of concrete and acts as a heat sink. Inside, the bright space is divided by exposed-concrete walls which radiate gentle heat like an enormous slow-burning stove in winter. The external appearance of the constructed glazing varies according to the weather conditions and the time of day, sometimes turning black with light iridescent reflections. Despite cloudy conditions in winter and a minimum of two and a half hours of sunshine, the total amount of thermal and electrical power required is entirely supplied by solar energy.

La Maison Solaire I est une maison à énergie zéro, construite dans la dépression du Rhin parallèlement à la vallée. Les capteurs de façade, opaques, situés à l'est, l'ouest et au sud, sont séparés par des fenêtres allant jusqu'à l'étage. Vu le faible apport énergétique au nord, il n'y a pas besoin d'accumulateur à cet endroit : cette condition est mise à profit par une fenêtre panoramique couvrant toute la façade nord. Le gros œuvre est réalisé en béton et sert d'accumulateur. A l'intérieur, l'espace est très clair et doté de murs en béton apparent, qui, en hiver, à l'instar d'un immense poêle de faïence, irradient une douce chaleur. L'apparence extérieure du verre employé pour la construction se modifie au gré des caprices atmosphériques et de l'heure de la journée : il est parfois noir, parfois doté de reflets clairs irisés. Malgré un horizon souvent nuageux en hiver et un ensoleillement minimal de 2,5 heures, le besoin total an énergie thermique et électrique est couvert par le rendement de l'énergie solaire.

Das Solarhaus I ist ein Nullenergiehaus und wurde in der Rheinsenkung parallel zum Tal hin erbaut. Die fassadenhohen, lichtundurchlässigen Kollektoren im Osten, Süden und Westen werden durch geschosshohe Fenster getrennt. Da der Energieeintrag im Norden sehr gering ist, wird dort kein Speicher benötigt; dieser Umstand wird genutzt, um so die gesamte Nordfassade als Lichtwand mit einem Panoramafenster auszugestalten. Der Rohbau ist in Beton ausgeführt und dient als Speicher. Im Innern entsteht ein heller Raum mit massiven Sichtbetonwänden, welche im Winter wie ein riesiger Kachelofen angenehme Strahlungswärme abgeben. Die äußere Erscheinung des zur Konstruktion verwendeten Glases, verändert sich je nach Wetterlage und Tageszeit, und ist mal schwarz, mal irisierend hell. Trotz starker Horizontverschattung im Winter, mit einer minimalen Sonnenscheindauer von 2,5 Stunden, wird der gesamte Bedarf an thermischer und elektrischer Energie durch die Sonnenenergienutzung gedeckt.

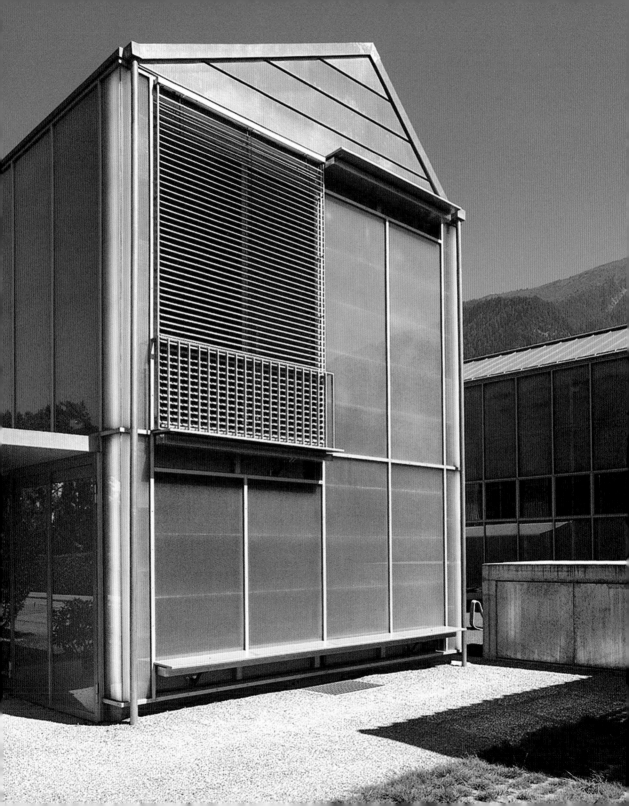

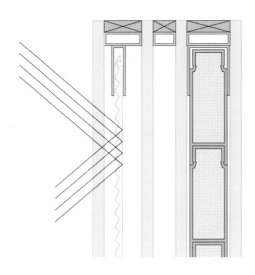

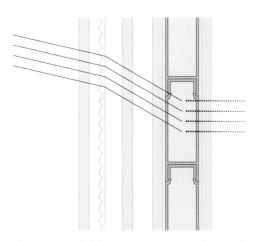

Construction details Détails de construction Konstruktionsdetails

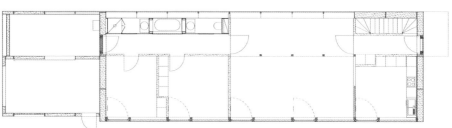

Ground floor Rez-de-chaussée Erdgeschoss

transparency makes glass the favorite material in solar-energy architecture. Here, the glass-covered façade is pure light, enhanced by a panoramic window.

t de sa transparence, le verre est le matériau par excellence dans l'architecture solaire. Il a été utilisé, pour la façade nord, tel un mur lumineux doté d'une fenêtre panoramique.

s ist als lichtdurchlässiges Material für die Solararchitektur prägend und wurde für die Nordfassade als Lichtwand mit einem Panoramafenster verwendet.

...posed concrete adds great warmth to the bright, pleasant interior, creating a welcoming atmosphere.

...s espaces intérieurs, clairs et agréables, habillés de béton apparent, dégagent une atmosphère chaleureuse.

...e Innenräume sind helle und ansprechende Räume, die mit massiven Sichtbetonwänden verkleidet sind, was eine warme Atmosphäre vermittelt.

☐ Watervilla

Architectuurstudio Herman Hertzberger

In few places is there such a tradition of floating houses, nor has the concept of the floating house been realized so often, as in the Netherlands. In this project the architects wanted to foster the sensation of independence and freedom that comes from living on the water. For this the architects devised a flexible construction system that would allow moving or turning the prototype with ease, making it possible to decide what views were wanted to delight the senses with or in what direction the sun was to shine on the house. This way a considerable energy savings is achieved because the home can absorb the solar energy during many hours of the day. The flotation system is composed of six interconnected cylinders made out of steel measuring two meters in diameter. To insure their durability and reduce maintenance they are constructed of ten millimeter thick metal. Relative to traditional concrete caissons, these elements have the advantage of being easily manageable and offering useful storage space.

Il y a peu d'endroits dotés d'une tradition si forte et où le concept de maison flottante a été étudié aussi intensément qu'aux Pays-bas. Avec ce projet, les architectes voulaient intensifier le sentiment d'indépendance et de liberté qu'offre la possibilité de vivre sur l'eau. Ils ont donc conçu un système de construction flexible qui permette de déplacer ou de tourner facilement le prototype. Ceci afin de déterminer les vues désirées et l'orientation de la maison par rapport au soleil. Cette méthode offre un gain d'énergie considérable, vu que l'habitation peut absorber l'énergie solaire tout au long de la journée. Le système de flottaison est constitué de six cylindres d'acier de deux mètres de diamètre reliés entre eux. Pour assurer sa durabilité et en réduire l'entretien, le choix s'est porté sur un métal de dix millimètres d'épaisseur. Par rapport aux caissons de béton traditionnels, ces éléments offrent l'avantage d'être facilement maniables et d'abriter en plus un espace de rangement utile.

Es gibt wenige Länder auf der Welt, in denen die Tradition schwimmender Häuser schon so lange besteht wie in den Niederlanden. Bei der Planung dieses Hauses sollte das Gefühl von Unabhängigkeit und Freiheit verstärkt werden, das das Leben auf dem Wasser gibt. Deshalb entwarfen die Architekten ein flexibles Konstruktionssystem, das es möglich macht, den Prototyp auf einfache Weise zu verlagern oder zu drehen, so dass die Bewohner sich den Ausblick oder die Richtung, aus der die Sonne ins Haus fallen soll, selber aussuchen können. So wird viel Energie gespart, da das Haus die Sonnenenergie tagsüber aufnehmen kann. Das Haus schwimmt auf einem System aus sechs Stahlzylindern mit einem Durchmesser von zwei Metern, die miteinander verbunden sind. Um die Haltbarkeit dieses Systems zu verlängern und den Instandhaltungsaufwand zu verringern, wählte man ein zehn Millimeter dickes Metall. Im Vergleich zu Beton haben diese Elemente den Vorteil, das sie einfach zu handhaben sind und zusätzlichen Lagerraum bieten.

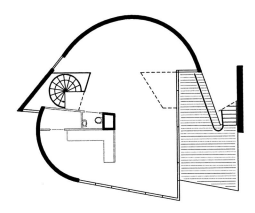

Lower level Niveau inférieur Untere Ebene

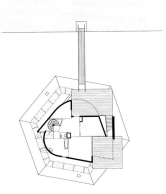

Ground floor Rez-de-chaussée Erdgeschoss

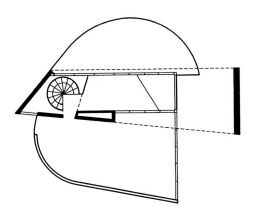

Upper level Niveau supérieur Obere Ebene

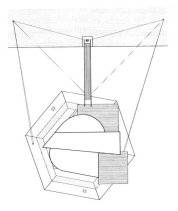

Roof plan Plan du toit Dachgeschoss

The sliding glass doors open up completely, allowing the sea breeze into the house.

Les portes de verre coulissantes s'ouvrent complètement, laissant la brise marine se répandre à flots dans toute la maison.

Die verglasten Schiebetüren lassen sich komplett öffnen und so kann die Meeresbrise durch den gesamten Wohnraum strömen.

Elevations Élévations Aufrisse

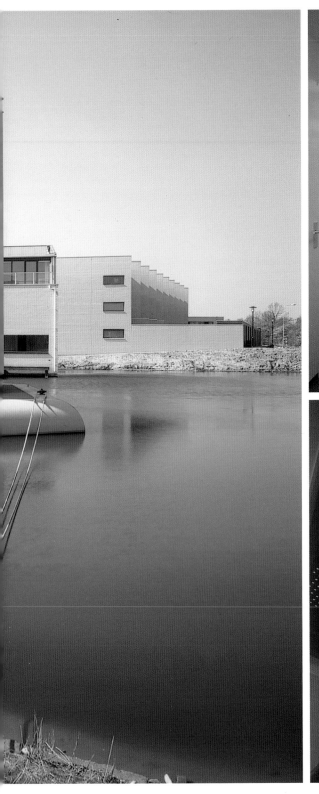

☐ Hendelkens Passive House

Maison Passive Hendelkens

Passivhaus Hendelkens

Rongen Architekten

Set on a rather sharp slope, this small detached house opens out towards the south and enjoys wonderful views of the surrounding countryside. The layout takes full advantage of the site, with the roof sloping opposite the bank allowing the great amount of natural light hitting the southern side to be used to heat the house as required. The architect had no trouble convincing his clients to build a 'passive house', a type of house with a low heating-energy consumption, making an 'active heating system' redundant. Thanks to this system, annual heating-energy consumption does not exceed 14.6kWh/m². The energy necessary for heating the house is produced by a wood chip burning stove. And a controlled ventilation system adds to the occupants' general comfort by providing a constant flow of renewed air with no draughts, a pleasant indoor temperature in the winter and fresh air in the summer.

Cette petite maison individuelle, implantée sur une pente escarpée, s'ouvre généreusement vers le sud, jouissant ainsi d'une merveilleuse vue donnant sur la nature. La topographie donnée permet d'optimiser le terrain : le toit s'élève donc adossé au talus, permettant de capter une grande quantité de lumière naturelle du côté sud pour obtenir suffisamment d'énergie solaire. L'architecte n'a pas eu de mal à persuader ses clients à construire une « maison passive ». C'est sa faible consommation d'énergie de chauffage qui caractérise ce type de maison, permettant de renoncer toute l'année à « un système de chauffage actif » d'où le nom de « maison passive ». Ceci permet d'avoir une consommation de chauffage annuelle ne dépassant pas 14,6 kWh/m². L'énergie de chauffage nécessaire est produite par un four à copeaux de bois. Le confort de la maison est accru par un système d'aération contrôlé : de l'air frais constant, pas de courants d'air, une température intérieure agréable en hiver et de l'air frais en été.

Das kleine Einfamilienwohnhaus liegt an einem Steilhang und öffnet sich uneingeschränkt nach Süden, wodurch ein herrlicher Ausblick in die freie Natur ermöglicht wird. Durch die gegebene Topographie kann das Grundstück optimal genutzt werden: das Dach erhebt sich entgegen dem Hang und durch das Licht auf der Südseite wird somit genügend solare Energie gewonnen. Der Architekt hatte wenig Mühe, die Bauherren-Familie davon zu überzeugen, ein ‚Passivhaus' zu bauen. Passivhäuser zeichnen sich insbesondere dadurch aus, dass sie nur so wenig Heizenergie benötigen, dass auf ein ‚aktives Heizsystem' ganzjährig verzichtet werden kann. Daher der Name ‚Passivhaus'. Dieses Passivhaus hat einen jährlichen Heizenergieverbrauch von nur 14,6 kWh/m². Die benötigte Heizenergie wird durch einen Holzpelletofen bereitgestellt. Der Wohnkomfort wird darüber hinaus noch durch eine kontrollierte Wohnungslüftungsanlage gesteigert: ständige Frischluft, keine Zugerscheinungen, angenehmes warmes Klima im Winter und frische, vorgekühlte Luft im Sommer.

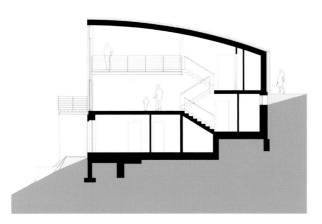

Section Section Schnitt

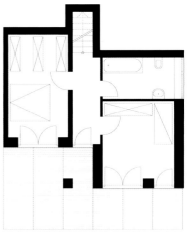

Ground floor Rez-de-chaussée Erdgeschoss

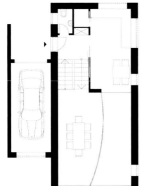

Lower level Niveau inférieur Untere Ebene

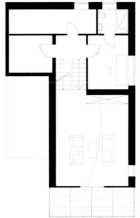

Upper level Niveau supérieur Obere Ebene

e roof slopes opposite the bank, making the most of the site and allowing a great amount of natural light to stream in on the southern side.

mpte tenu de la topographie, le toit s'élève contre la pente, permettant de capter une grande quantité de lumière sur le côté sud.

rch die gegebene Topographie erhebt sich das Dach entgegen dem Hang, was dazu führt, dass besonders viel Licht auf der Südseite eingefangen wird.

Stormanns Passive House

Maison Passive Stormanns

Passivhaus Stormanns

Rongen Architekten

Heating-energy consumption of this house, built in accordance with 'passive house' standards, is 80% lower than that of a low-energy-consumption house, making it clear that energy efficiency plays an important part in its architecture. On the one hand, a controlled ventilation system with efficient heat recovery can provide a pleasant ambient temperature, even during the coldest months of the year, while reducing the need for the back-up heating system. On the other hand, the air quality is perfect from the point of view of health. A system of solar panels installed on the roof supplies both hot water for general use and heating. The erection of external walls is crucial as the solid cellular concrete used has a great heat- retention capacity with added thermal insulation. Untreated larch wood panels with a grey-varnish coating cover the northern façade, as durable as roughcast or stone walls and requiring little maintenance.

Cette maison, construite selon les normes de maison passive, consomme 80% de moins d'énergie de chauffage qu'une habitation à basse énergie et prouve que le thème « réduire la consommation d'énergie » offre un potentiel considérable en architecture. D'une part, un système de ventilation contrôlée, avec récupération de chaleur, veille à ne devoir utiliser qu'un faible chauffage d'appoint, pour doter la maison, même au plus froid de l'hiver, d'une température ambiante agréable. D'autre part, la qualité de l'air est toujours parfaite sur le plan hygiène. Un système de capteurs solaires installés sur le toit permet de chauffer l'eau pour l'usage courant et assure le chauffage. La construction des murs extérieurs est d'importance : en effet, ils sont constitués de béton cellulaire massif d'une grande capacité de captage et doté d'isolation thermique. La façade nord de la maison est habillée de lattes de bois de mélèze non traité, vernis en gris, nécessitant peu d'entretien et d'une durabilité qui ne cède en rien aux façades en crépis ou en pierre.

Dieses nach Passivhausstandard gebaute Wohnhaus verbraucht ca. 80% weniger Heizenergie als ein Niedrigenergiehaus und liefert den Beweis, dass das Thema "Energiesparen" in der Architektur ein großes Potential darstellt. Auf der einen Seite sorgt eine kontrollierte Lüftungsanlage mit Wärmerückgewinnung dafür, dass nur ein äußerst geringer Restwärmebedarf sichergestellt werden muss, um das Haus selbst im tiefsten Winter auf angenehme Raumtemperaturen zu bringen. Auf der anderen Seite ist die Luftqualität allzeit von allerhöchster Hygiene gekennzeichnet. Eine Solarkollektoranlage auf dem Dach dient der Brauchwassererwärmung und der Heizungsunterstützung. Wesentlich war die Konstruktion der Außenwände, die aus massiven, speicherfähigen Porenbetonwänden mit zusätzlicher Wärmedämmung bestehen. Die Nordfassade des Hauses wurde mit grau lasierten, unbehandelten Lärchenholzleisten verschalt, die absolut wartungsfrei sind und einer Putz- oder Steinfassade in ihrer Lebensdauer um nichts nach stehen.

The cozy atmosphere of this house is due partly to the additional thermal insulation provided by the solid cellular-concrete walls.

Le bâtiment dégage une atmosphère douillette. Les murs massifs en béton cellulaire complètent également l'isolation thermique.

Mit seiner roten Putzfassade strahlt das Gebäude eine behagliche Atmosphäre aus. Diese massiven Porenbetonwände dienen zur zusätzlicher Wärmedämmung.

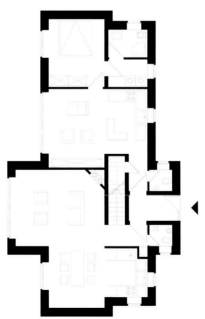

Ground floor Rez-de-chaussée Erdgeschoss

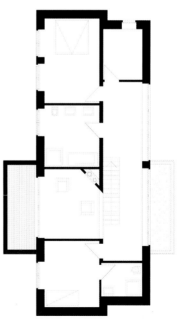

First floor Premier étage Erstes Obergeschoss

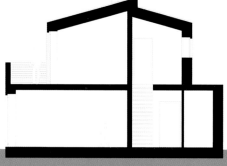

Section Section Schnitt

Engels-Houben Passive House
Maison Passive Engels-Houben
Passivhaus Engels-Houben

Rongen Architekten

The site chosen for the house is located in the heart of the Wurmtal leisure park, bordered by a garden and a small river to the west. The exterior of the house has been designed in harmony with the site and takes the height of the sun into account. While its northern and eastern sides are rather restricted, the building opens out towards the south and the east, with views of the garden and the landscape. This detached house meets the standards of a 'passive house', which means a house with an annual heating consumption not exceeding 14.6 kWh/m^2. The remaining energy necessary is provided by a wood-chip burning stove which constitutes the only back-up heating system. As the basic yearly energy requirement of the house is 74.9 kWh/m^2, the project managers chose a solar-cell installation linked to a 750-litre tank for both water-heating and back-up heating, meeting the occupants' year-round hot-water needs.

Le terrain à construire est situé au coeur de la zone de parc et loisir du Wurmtal. Il est délimité sur le coté ouest par un jardin et une petite rivière. L'extérieur de la maison est conçu en fonction du site et de la hauteur du soleil sur le terrain. Alors que les côtés est et nord semblent plutôt fermés, le bâtiment s'ouvre généreusement vers le sud et l'ouest sur le jardin et le paysage. Cette maison individuelle a été construite pour répondre aux normes d'une maison passive, ce qui signifie que sa consommation annuelle en énergie de chauffage ne dépasse pas 14,6 kWh/m². L'énergie restante nécessaire provient uniquement d'un four à petits bois, seul système de chauffage d'appoint. Le besoin primaire en énergie de la maison représente 74,9 kWh/m² par an. Par conséquent les maîtres de l'ouvrage ont opté pour une installation à capteurs solaires reliés à un réservoir de 750 litres tant pour réchauffer l'eau chaude que comme chauffage d'appoint. Cette installation permet aux habitants de couvrir eux-mêmes leur besoin annuel en eau chaude.

Das Baugrundstück liegt mitten im Naherholungsgebiet Wurmtal und wird auf der Westseite durch einen Garten und einen kleinen Fluss begrenzt. Die äußere Gestaltung des Hauses reagiert sowohl auf die Lage als auch auf den Sonnenstand auf dem Grundstück. Während Nord- und Ostseite eher geschlossen wirken, öffnet sich das Gebäude großzügig nach Süden und Westen zum Garten und zur Landschaft hin. Das Einfamilienhaus wurde im Passivhausstandard gebaut, das bedeutet, dass es im Jahr nur 14,6 kWh/m² an Heizenergie verbraucht. Die benötigte Restenergie wird über einen Stückholzofen als einziges Heizsystem bereitgestellt. Der Primärenergiebedarf des Hauses liegt bei 74,9 kWh/m² pro Jahr. Darüber hinaus entschieden sich die Bauherren auch für eine eigene Solarkollektoranlage mit einem angeschlossenen 750 Liter Speichertank zur Erwärmung des Warmwassers und zur Heizungsunterstützung. Diese Anlage ermöglicht es den Bewohnern den größten Teil des Jahres ihren Warmwasserbedarf selbst abzudecken.

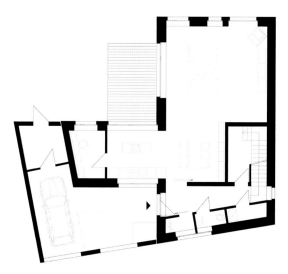

Ground floor Rez-de-chaussée Erdgeschoss

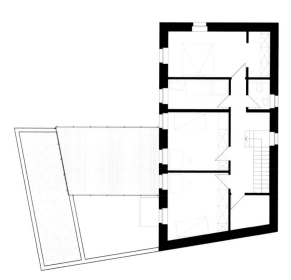

First floor Premier étage Erstes Obergeschoss

While its northern and eastern sides are rather restricted, the building opens out towards the south and east onto a small garden.

Si les côtés nord et est semblent plutôt fermés, en revanche, le bâtiment s'ouvre généreusement vers le sud et l'ouest sur le petit jardin.

Während Nord- und Ostseite eher geschlossen wirken, öffnet sich das Gebäude großzügig nach Süden und Westen zu dem kleinen Garten hin.

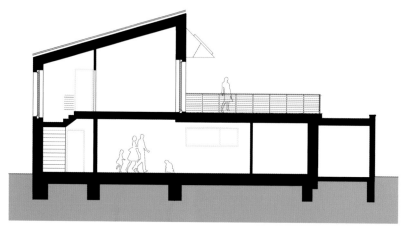

Longitudinal section Section longitudinale Längsschnitt

☐ Solar Residence Complex
Lotissement Solaire
Solarsiedlung

Rolf Disch

The house of the future is no longer an impossible dream. It has become an essential element of cities and regions, offering a unique living experience based on high-quality housing thanks to the global concept and use of renewable energies. The Solar Residence Complex takes natural resources into account, be it in the architectural design, in the choice of building materials or in the water and energy system selected. A practical and attractive design does not only encourage the residents' creativity, but also represents considerable cost savings. Environment-friendly mobility is also made possible by a public transport system and a network of footpaths and bicycle paths connecting the different areas of the complex based on the judicious interaction of its various elements.

La maison du futur n'est plus une utopie mais réalisable dès maintenant. Il fait partie du lotissement de la ville, de la région, offrant à ses habitants un concept global d'utilisation d'énergies renouvelables, ainsi qu'une expérience de vie conjuguant à la fois une grande qualité d'habitat et de vie. Que ce soit dans le concept architectural, le choix des matériaux de construction ou du système de l'eau et de l'énergie, le lotissement solaire tient compte des ressources naturelles. Conception et esthétique favorisent la créativité des habitants, la diminution des charges et dépenses épargnant leur porte-monnaie. En outre, ils bénéficient d'une mobilité respectueuse de l'environnement grâce aux moyens de transports en commun et au réseau de voies piétonnes et cyclistes. Tous les différents domaines du lotissement étant reliés entre eux, il en découle une interaction judicieuse des composantes les plus diverses.

Das Haus der Zukunft ist keine Utopie mehr sondern jetzt realisierbar. Es ist Bestandteil der Siedlung, der Stadt, der Region und bietet seinem Bewohner ein ganzheitliches Konzept zur Nutzung regenerativer Energien, sowie ein kommunikatives Wohnerlebnis mit gleichzeitiger hoher Wohn- und Aufenthaltsqualität. Sowohl im Baukonzept, in der Auswahl der Baumaterialien als auch in Wasser- und Energiesystemen werden in der Solarsiedlung die natürlichen Ressourcen berücksichtigt. Gestaltung und Ästhetik fördern die Kreativität der Bewohner, die Nebenkosten und Aufwendungen bleiben gering, während die gute Anbindung an das öffentliche Verkehrs-, wie auch Fuß- und Radwegenetz, umweltfreundliche Mobilität gewährleistet. Indem die verschiedenen Bereiche der Siedlung ineinander greifen, ereignet sich ein sinnvolles Zusammenspiel der unterschiedlichsten Komponenten.

use of natural materials gives the interior a warm radiant atmosphere.

pace intérieur, bénéficiant également de matériaux naturels, dégage une ambiance radieuse et chaleureuse.

h in den Innenräumen wurde auf die Verwendung natürlicher Materialien geachtet und so entsteht ein hell und freundlich wirkendes Ambiente.

☐ Fujy Home
Habitation Fujy
Haus Fujy

Fujy naturally architecture

The pilot project of Fujy naturally architecture is a sustainable single-family designer home with the latest technical advances. It uses safe and renewable materials, finishings and interior furniture such as the certified wood structure. To promote energy savings, the project integrates different passive systems such as insulation by inertia thanks to the use of thermal-acoustic bricks around the entire exterior perimeter of the house, carpentry with thermal bridge rupture, or the single-layer, natural waterproofing. The house also has solar panels, electrical glow grills for the rooms and thermal windows. The Fujy house produces its own thermal energy through solar panels and complements it with a high-performance electronic modular condensation boiler.

Le projet pilote de Fujy naturally architecture présente une habitation individuelle durable, très design et dotée des derniers progrès technologiques. Les matériaux, finitions et meubles d'intérieur sont sûrs et renouvelables à l'instar de la structure en bois certifié. Pour maximaliser le gain d'énergie, le projet intègre divers systèmes passifs comme l'isolation par inertie grâce à l'emploi de briques thermo- acoustiques sur tout le périmètre extérieur de la maison, la menuiserie avec rupture de pont thermique, ou la couche unique de revêtement hydrofuge naturel. La maison dispose également de lames de contrôle solaire, grilles électriques de préchauffage des pièces et verres thermiques. La maison Fujy produit sa propre énergie thermique grâce aux panneaux solaires complétés par une chaudière électronique modulante à condensation à haut rendement.

Das Pilotprojekt des Architekten Fujy naturally architecture, ist ein nachhaltiges Haus, das nach den neusten Technologien entworfen wurde. Es wurden sichere und erneuerbare Materialien, Flächen und Möbel benutzt, ein Beispiel dafür ist die Struktur aus Holz mit Umweltzertifikat. Um so viel Energie wie möglich zu sparen, wurden verschiedene passive Systeme zur Isolierung benutzt wie zum Beispiel die Steine zur thermischen und akustischen Isolierung, aus der alle Außenwände sind, die Fenster- und Türrahmen, die die Wärmebrücken unterbrechen, und die natürliche, einschichtige und feuchtigkeitsbeständige Verkleidung. Ebenso wurde das Haus mit Lamellen zur Kontrolle der Sonne, mit elektrischen, vorheizbaren Gittern für die Räume und mit Thermoglas ausgestattet. Das Haus Fujy produziert seine eigene Wärmeenergie mithilfe von Solarplatten. Dieses System wird durch einen hocheffizienten, elektronisch gesteuerten Kondensationsboiler mit modulierbarem Betrieb ergänzt.

Site plan Plan de situation Umgebungsplan

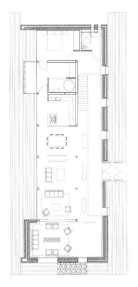

Ground floor Rez-de-chaussée Erdgeschoss

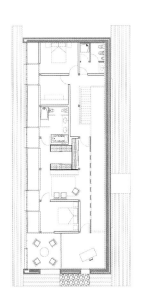

First floor Premier étage Erstes Obergeschoss

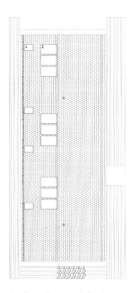

Roof plan Plan du toit Dachgeschoss

The combination of natural wood and high white walls gives the main living space a brightness and openness emphasized by the natural light coming in directly through the roof window.

L'alliance de bois naturel et de hauts murs blancs confère à l'espace de vie clarté et ouverture. La lumière du jour entre directement dans les pièces par la fenêtre de toit.

Die Kombination von Naturholz und hohen weißen Wänden lässt die Räume hell und offen wirken. Tageslicht fällt durch das Dachfenster direkt in den Wohnraum.

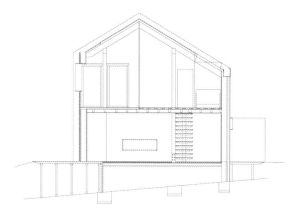
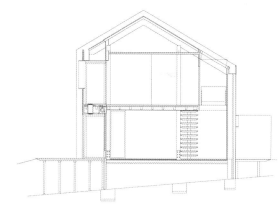

Sections Sections Schnitte

□ CO$_2$ Balance Dwellings

Pavillons CO$_2$ Balance

CO$_2$ Balance Wohnhäuser

J. P. Moehrlein, MAD Moehrleinvandelft

This complex consists of 15 houses and is one of the first projects carried out in the Netherlands that meet the requirements of 'CO$_2$-neutral buildings'. While designing it, the architects focused on the development of bioclimatic construction systems within the 'sustainable building' framework, which involves energy-efficiency through the active and passive use of solar energy. The orientation of the sun and the use of sound-proofing were decisive factors in the choice of location, off ringroad 32, and in the layout of the interior spaces. Another important aspect of the design is the integration of an unusual system of domestic installations which includes, among other things, the construction of a south-facing photovoltaic-paneled roof, acting as a solar-energy collector to make optimum use of this energy. Other features of sustainable buildings are the installation of heating systems under the floors and in heat-radiating walls and the use of damp-proofing on external walls.

Ce lotissement, projet comprenant 15 habitations, est l'un des premiers aux Pays-bas à remplir les conditions liées à « la neutralité en CO₂ ». Par ailleurs, les architectes ont attaché une grande importance au développement des techniques énergétiques et de construction relatives à la « construction durable », garantissant également la réduction de consommation d'énergie par le biais du système d'énergie solaire passive et active. Dans la distribution intérieure des espaces de vie, deux aspects ont été déterminants : l'orientation vers le soleil et l'isolation phonique visant à parer aux nuisances sonores liées à la déviation N32. Autre élément notoire du projet, l'intégration des installations techniques qui conduit, entre autres, à une forme de toit spécifique orienté vers le sud visant à optimiser l'utilisation des capteurs solaires des habitations. L'installation d'un chauffage au sol et mural et la création d'une façade saine qui laisse passer l'humidité, sont autant de manifestations visibles de la construction durable.

Bei dieser Wohnsiedlung handelt es sich um ein 15 Wohnhäuser umfassendes Projekt, das als eines der ersten in den Niederlanden die Bedingung 'CO₂-neutrale Ausführung' erfüllt. Darüber hinaus legten die Architekten großen Wert darauf, die Energie- und Bautechnik im Rahmen des Themas „Nachhaltiges Bauen" weiterzuentwickeln und die Energieeinsparung durch Verwendung aktiver und passiver Sonnenenergiesysteme zu gewährleisten. Die Ausrichtung zur Sonne einerseits und die Lärmbelastung durch die Umgehungsstraße N32 andererseits waren somit ausschlaggebend für die interne Aufteilung der Wohnfunktionen. Ein weiterer Aspekt des Entwurfs war die Integration der Anlagentechnik, die unter anderem zu einer spezifischen, nach Süden ausgerichteten Dachform führte, durch die die Sonnenkollektoren für die Wohnungen optimal nutzbar sind. Der Aspekt des Nachhaltigen Bauens manifestiert sich außerdem in der Installation von Wand- und Bodenheizungen und in der Vermeidung einer dampfdichten Fassade.

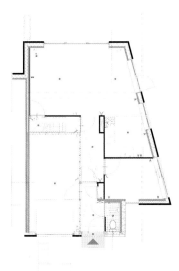

Ground floor Rez-de-chaussée Erdgeschoss

First floor Premier étage Erstes Obergeschoss

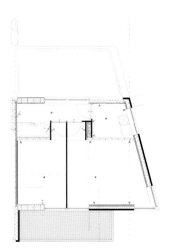

Second floor Deuxième étage Zweites Obergeschoss

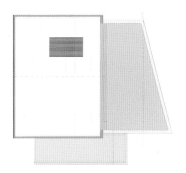

Roof plan Plan du toit Dachgeschoss

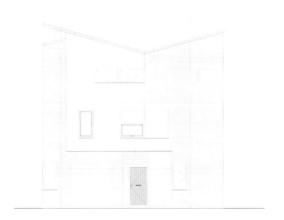

Front elevation Elévation frontale Vorderansicht

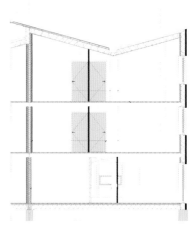

Longitudinal section Section longitudinale Längsschnitt

Rear elevation Élévation arrière Hinteransicht

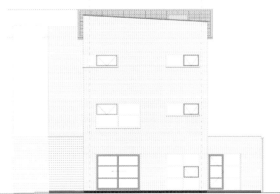

Side elevation Élévation latérale Seitenansicht

ous ecological issues have been taken into account, along with the use of clean lines in the design of this residential complex.

réation de ce lotissement s'est faite en tenant compte de divers aspects écologiques liés à un design épuré.

Errichtung dieser Wohnsiedlung wurden unterschiedliche ökolgische Aspekte mit einem zeitgenössischen und schlichten Design vereint.

Elevations Élévations Aufrisse

☐ Solar Tube House
Maison Solar Tube
Solar Tube Haus

Driendl* Architects

Before the actual design process of this project could be started, the characteristics of the location, the plot and the landscape had to be checked accurately. The sun's position needed to be taken into account as well as the number of hours of sunlight and a range of other weather aspects. The idea was to use the entire house as a solar collector which needs only little heating, cooling or electric illumination. A complex low energy concept was designed which includes a special ventilation system that works like a chimney to cool the house. The atrium allows heat to travel upwards to be expelled at the roof level trough an opening panel. On the other hand the defoliated trees in winter allow the sunlight to shine through the glazed facade and roof and therefore also help cutting the heating costs.

Avant de démarrer la conception du projet, il a fallu vérifier soigneusement les données de l'emplacement, du terrain et du paysage : tenir compte également de la position du soleil, du nombre d'heures d'ensoleillement et de toute une série de données climatiques. L'idée de base est d'utiliser toute la maison comme un collecteur solaire, nécessitant peu de chauffage, climatisation ou éclairage électrique. Un concept complexe de basse énergie a donc été conçu comprenant un système spécial de ventilation qui fonctionne comme une cheminée – grâce à l'atrium, la chaleur s'élève pour s'échapper au niveau du toit par un panneau ouvert. Par ailleurs, les arbres dépouillés de feuilles en hiver laissent passer le soleil à travers les vitrages des façades et du toit permettant aussi de réduire les coûts de chauffage.

Bevor man wirklich mit dem Planungsprozess beginnen konnte, mussten die Charakteristika des Standorts, das Grundstück und die Landschaft sorgfältig analysiert werden. Die Position der Sonne, die täglichen Sonnenstunden und verschiedene andere Aspekte des Wetters wurden vor der eigentlichen Gestaltung des Hauses beobachtet. Man wollte das ganze Haus als Sonnenkollektor benutzen, um so mit weniger Heizung, Kühlung und elektrischer Beleuchtung auszukommen. Ein komplexes Niedrigenergiekonzept wurde geschaffen, zu dem ein speziell entworfenes Belüftungssystem gehört, das wie ein Schornstein funktioniert. Die Wärme steigt durch den Vorhof aufwärts und wird auf Höhe des Daches durch ein sich öffnendes Paneel ausgestoßen. Im Winter hingegen lassen die blätterlosen Bäume das Licht durch die verglaste Fassade und das Dach fallen, so dass die Heizkosten gesenkt werden.

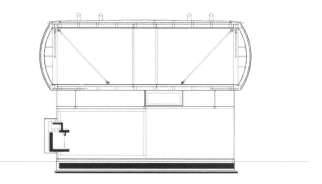

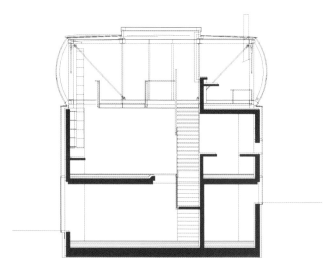

Sections Sections Schnitte

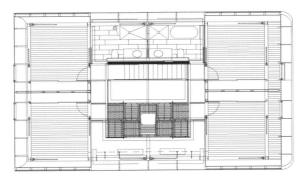

Ground floor Rez-de-chaussée Erdgeschoss

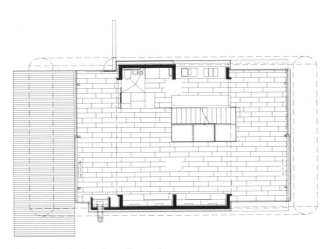

First floor Premier étage Erstes Obergeschoss

Glass, as an almost unique building material, makes interior spaces seem to blend naturally with the natural surroundings.

Le verre, en tant que matériau de construction presque unique, donne l'impression que l'espace intérieur se fond à l'environnement.

Glas als überwiegend verwendetes Konstruktionsmaterial vermittelt den Eindruck, als ob Innenraum und Umgebung miteinander verschmelzen.

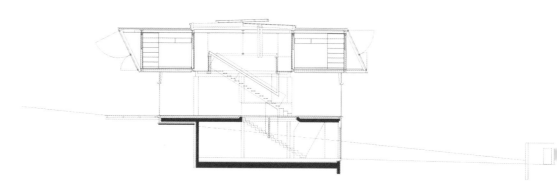

Longitudinal section Section longitudinale Längsschnitt

Gregóire-Opdebeeck House
Maison Gregóire-Opdebeeck
Gregóire-Opdebeeck Haus

Marc Opdebeeck

This home, a renovation of an old industrial laundry, is supported by the concept of energy sustainability, something that is achieved through the application of highly insulating materials, such as wood on the upper floors and the façades, and that are resistant to the passing of time, such as the ceramic pavement of the living room. It minimizes the use of fuel for heating. Similarly, the light tone zinc covering paint and openings to the exterior that have been made between the walls and the roof contribute to creating a cool atmosphere in summer. The house is heated by solar energy supplemented by wood burning and a small percentage of natural gas. Thanks to investment in technical advances in insulation and energy savings, this house is already adapted to the future need for decrease use of fossil energy.

Cette maison, fruit de la restauration d'une ancienne blanchisserie industrielle, s'appuie sur le concept d'énergie durable, grâce à l'utilisation de matériaux hautement isolants, comme le bois, pour les niveaux supérieurs et les façades, et résistants dans le temps comme les carrelages en céramique de l'espace de vie. L'emploi de combustibles pour le chauffage est minimisé. Dans le même esprit, la toiture en zinc peint d'une couleur claire et les ouvertures sur l'extérieur réalisées entre les murs et le toit contribuent à rafraîchir l'ambiance en été. La maison fonctionne grâce à l'énergie solaire, complétée par la combustion du bois et d'un faible pourcentage de gaz naturel. Convertie aux techniques de pointe en matière d'isolation et de gain d'énergie, cette maison est déjà adaptée pour faire face aux futures diminutions de la consommation d'énergies fossiles.

Eine ehemalige Industriewäscherei wurde zu einem energetisch nachhaltigen Wohnhaus umgebaut. Dazu wurden Materialien mit hohem Isolationsvermögen und einer langen Haltbarkeit benutzt wie das Holz in den oberen Stockwerken und an der Fassade, und Keramikfußböden in den Aufenthaltsbereichen. Der Kraftstoffverbrauch für die Heizung wird soweit wie möglich reduziert. Ebenso tragen das Dach aus hell gestrichenem Zink und die Fenster zwischen den Wänden und dem Dach dazu bei, im Sommer für Kühle zu sorgen. Das Haus funktioniert mit Solarenergie, unterstützt durch die Verbrennung von Holz und einem kleinem Anteil an Gas. Aufgrund der Investition in fortschrittliche Technologien im Bereich der Isolierung und des Energiesparens ist dieses Haus für den Fall vorbereitet, dass in der Zukunft noch mehr fossile Energien gespart werden müssen.

Front elevation Elévation frontale Vorderansicht   Rear elevation Élévation arrière Hinteransicht

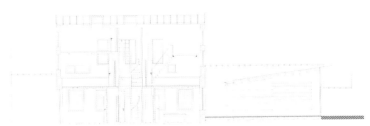

Sections Sections Schnitte

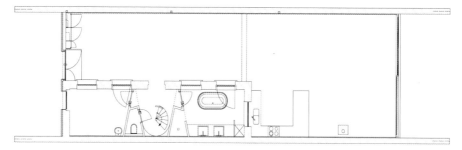

Ground floor Rez-de-chaussée Erdgeschoss

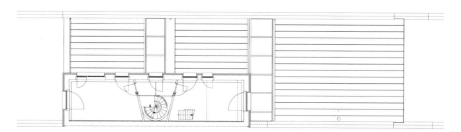

First floor Premier étage Erstes Obergeschoss

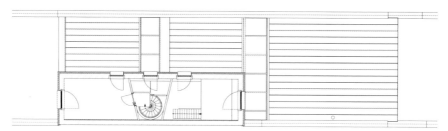

Second floor Deuxième étage Zweites Obergeschoss

The interior space is open-plan. Wood-paneling has been used in the kitchen and bathroom, as well as on some furnishings.

Les espaces intérieurs affichent un plan ouvert. Le bois se retrouve dans l'habillage de la cuisine et de la salle de bains ainsi que sur certains meubles.

Die Innenräume sind von einem offenen Grundriss geprägt. Holz wurde sowohl für die Küchen- und Badverkleidung verwendet als auch für einzelnen Möbelstücke.

Wine Creek Road Residence
Residence de la Wine Creek Road
Wine Creek Road Residenz

Siegel & Stein Architects

The aim of this project was to build an energy efficient and sustainable house, taking into account the small dimensions of the parcel and at the same time maximize the feeling of space and openness. The architects decided to build the residence on the upper edge of the site to preserve the meadow below and maximize views beyond. A careful site analysis determined that the steep hills to the west and south limited year-round solar access. This condition eliminated the possibility of passive solar heating but on the other hand opened the possibility to keep the house cool in summer without mechanical cooling, which lead the design team to use that factor as the principal strategy for saving energy. This was accomplished by employing natural ventilation, superior insulation, and thermal mass. A high efficiency water heater provides radiant floor heating while the applied materials were selected for durability and ease of maintenance.

Ce projet vise à construire une maison durable à efficacité appelée « éconergétique », en tenant compte de la dimension réduite du terrain tout en maximisant le sentiment d'espace et d'ouverture. Les architectes ont décidé de construire la résidence tout en haut du site pour préserver le pré au-dessous et maximaliser les vues. Une analyse détaillée du site a permis de constater que la pente des collines ouest et sud limitait l'ensoleillement annuel. Cette condition éliminait d'office l'utilisation possible d'un chauffage solaire, mais permettait par ailleurs de garder la maison fraîche en été sans climatisation, conduisant l'équipe de concepteurs à utiliser ce facteur comme stratégie principale d'économie d'énergie. Ceci en employant la ventilation naturelle, l'isolation supérieure et la masse thermique. Un chauffe-eau à haute énergie alimente un chauffage au sol par rayonnement, avec des matériaux sélectionnés pour leur durabilité et facilité d'entretien.

Das Ziel dieses Bauvorhabens war es, ein Energiesparhaus zu bauen, das trotz der geringen Grundstücksgröße offen und weit wirkt. Die Architekten beschlossen, das Haus an der oberen Grundstücksgrenze zu errichten, um die Wiese darunter zu erhalten um einen weiten Ausblick zu schaffen. Eine gründliche Analyse des Grundstücks führte zu dem Ergebnis, dass die steilen Hügel im Westen und Süden den Sonneneinfall im Laufe des Jahres behindern. Dadurch wurde die passive Solarbeheizung unmöglich gemacht, aber andererseits ergab sich die Möglichkeit, das Haus im Sommer ohne ein mechanisches Kühlsystem zu kühlen. Deshalb beschlossen die Planer, diesen Faktor als wichtigste Strategie zum Einsparen von Energie zu nutzen. Man erreichte dies durch natürliche Belüftung, obere Isolierung und thermale Masse. Ein hocheffizienter Wasserboiler versorgt die Fußbodenheizung und die verwendeten Materialien wurden nach Haltbarkeit und einfacher Instandhaltung ausgewählt.

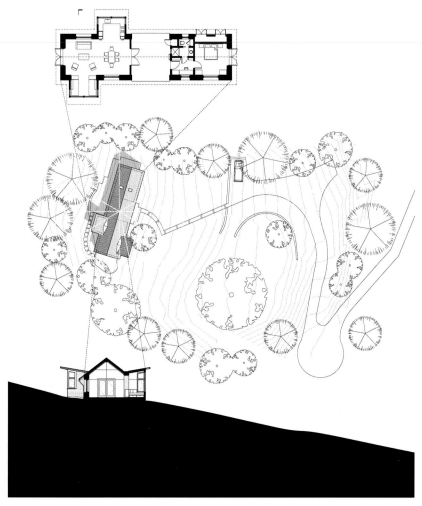

Plan Plan Grundriss

The glass front door is a direct link to the exterior, making it possible to enjoy the beautiful landscape beyond it from the main entrance.

La porte en verre de l'entrée principale permet au regard de musarder dans la merveilleuse nature alentour, créant ainsi un lien direct entre l'espace intérieur et extérieur.

Die verglaste Haupteingangstüre gibt den Blick auf die herrliche Umgebung frei und stellt die direkte Verbindung zwischen Innen- und Außenbereich dar.

The terrace offers breathtaking views over Dry Creek Valley and its vineyards.

Depuis la terrasse, les occupants bénéficient d'une vue époustouflante sur les vignobles qui couvrent la vallée de Dry Creek.

Von der Terasse aus läßt sich die atemberaubende Aussicht auf die im Dry Creek Tal gelegenen Weinberge genießen.

Rubissow Farmhouse
Ferme Rubissow
Rubissow Farmhaus

Okamoto Saijo Architecture

This project was designed as a case study within a wide ranging research project about green design, sustainability and urban ecology, conducted by Okamoto Saijo Architecture and other visionary architects. The farmhouse combines various basic ecological features under one roof. Starting with the improvement of solar exposure, the major rooms are oriented to the south. Operable windows are located in strategic places for natural cross ventilation while the eaves overhanging the south facing windows are designed to shade the summer sun, but allow the winter sun to enter the building. A radiant floor heating system is powered by the water heater, using solar energy. Another main ecological building aspect is the usage of recycled and sustainable building materials. An elaborated cellulose insulation system is built from newspapers and old blue jeans while the redwood doors are made from an old water tank.

Ce projet fait partie d'une étude de cas dans le cadre d'un vaste projet de recherche sur « l'écoconception », la préservation de l'environnement et l'écologie urbaine, dirigé par Okamoto Saijo Architecture et d'autres architectes visionnaires. La ferme réunit diverses caractéristiques écologiques de base sous un toit. Tout d'abord, les pièces principales sont orientées plein sud, afin d'améliorer l'exposition solaire. Les fenêtres mobiles sont placées à des endroits stratégiques pour une ventilation transversale naturelle. Ensuite, les avant-toits surplombent les fenêtres situées plein sud, les protégeant du soleil, tout en laissant entrer le soleil d'hiver. Un système de chauffage au sol radiant est alimenté par le chauffe-eau, utilisant l'énergie solaire. Dans cette ferme, l'emploi de matériaux de construction recyclés et durables est un autre aspect écologique essentiel. Un système d'isolation à base de cellulose est réalisé à partir de journaux et de vieux jeans tandis que les portes rouges, faites sur mesure, sont fabriquées à partir d'un vieux réservoir d'eau.

Dieses Gebäude entstand als Fallstudie innerhalb eines umfassenden Forschungsprojektes zur, Nachhaltigkeit und urbaner Ökologie, das von dem Studio Okamato Saijo Architecture und weiteren Architekten durchgeführt wurde. In diesem Bauernhaus werden verschiedene, grundlegende ökologische Eigenschaften unter einem Dach kombiniert. Zunächst wurde die Sonneneinstrahlung optimiert, indem die größeren Räume in Richtung Süden orientiert wurden. Die beweglichen Fenster sind an strategisch günstigen Stellen angebracht, um eine überkreuzte Belüftung zu ermöglichen. Die Dachtraufen der Südfenster hängen über, um im Sommer Schatten zu spenden. Die Fußbodenheizung wird über einen Wasserboiler mit Solarenergie betrieben. Ein anderer wichtiger Umweltaspekt ist die Benutzung von wieder verwertetem und umweltfreundlichem Baumaterial. Man entwarf in sorgfältiger Planung ein Zellulose-Isoliersystem aus Zeitungspapier und altem Jeansstoff, und die maßgearbeiteten Türen aus Rotholz wurden mit einem alten Wassertank konstruiert.

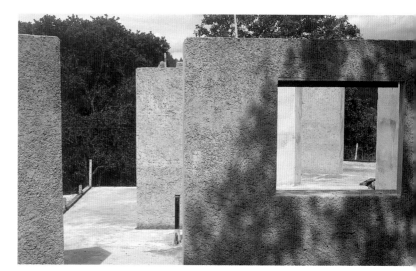

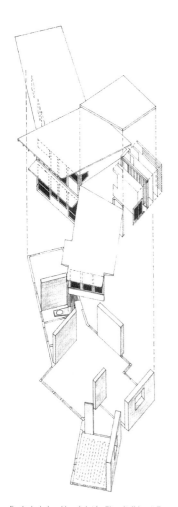

Exploded view Vue éclatée Einzelteildarstellung

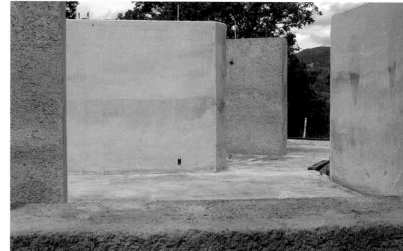

judicious and strategic positioning of windows makes for perfect natural ventilation and the optimum use of daylight.

Judicieux agencement des fenêtres suit un ordre stratégique, assurant ainsi une parfaite ventilation naturelle et une optimisation de l'usage de la lumière du jour.

Anordnung der Fenster ist strategisch durchdacht um die bestmögliche natürliche Belüftung und die maximale Ausnutzung des Tageslichtes zu garantieren.

☐ Solar House III

Maison Solaire III

Solarhaus III

GLASSX AG, Dietrich Schwarz

Solar House III was designed as a zero-energy house with low construction costs. In 2001 it received the Prix Solaire Suisse award thanks to its extensive 474-square-foot solar wall especially created and developped by the architects. The latent accumulator is crucial to this invention and its distinctive feature is the material it contains: a special type of paraffin which melts and freezes according to the ambient temperature. Solar energy recharges the accumulator mass, followed after a short interval by the distribution of thermal energy, providing the house with pleasant radiant heat. Apart from its practical advantages, this solar surface is also quite attractive as the brightness of the wall interacts very well with the surrounding environment. A small, efficient air pump provides mechanical ventilation, making full use of the outcoming airflow.

La maison solaire III a été conçue comme maison à énergie zéro avec un faible coût de construction. En 2001, elle a reçu le Prix Solaire Suisse, grâce au grand mur solaire de 44 m², spécialement inventé et exploité par le bureau d'architecture. Ce qui est essentiel dans cette invention, c'est l'accumulateur latent. Sa particularité réside dans la matière qu'il contient : dans ce cas précis, une paraffine spéciale qui fond et gèle à température ambiante. L'énergie solaire recharge d'abord la masse de l'accumulateur, avant que l'énergie thermique soit distribuée à l'intérieur, avec un décalage, sous forme de chaleur irradiante agréable. Outres ses avantages physiques, cette paroi solaire présente un intérêt esthétique certain. L'interaction de l'environnement extérieur est perceptible grâce à la clarté du mur. La ventilation mécanique se fait par le biais d'une petite pompe à chaleur à air/air efficace, de telle sorte que l'énergie restante de l'air sortant est totalement utilisée.

Das Solarhaus III wurde mit sehr geringen Gebäudekosten als Nullenergiehaus konzipiert und erhielt 2001 für die von dem Architekturbüro eigens entwickelte und patentierte Erfindung einer 44 m² grossen Solarwand den Schweizer Solarpreis. Wegweisend an dieser Erfindung ist der Latentspeicher. Dieser hat die Eigenschaft, dass das eingeschlossene Material, in diesem Fall ein spezielles Paraffin, bei Raumtemperatur schmilzt und gefriert. Die solare Energie lädt zuerst die Speichermasse auf, bevor die thermische Energie als angenehme Strahlungswärme mit einer Phasenverschiebung an den Innenraum abgegeben wird. Diese Solarwand hat neben den physikalischen Vorteilen auch einen ausgesprochen ästhetischen Reiz. Die Interaktion mit der Außenwelt wird im Innenraum durch die Helligkeit der Wand spürbar. Die mechanische Lüftung wird durch eine kleine, effiziente Luft-Luft-Wärmepumpe ergänzt, so dass die restliche Energie der Fortluft völlig ausgeschöpft wird.

This house has benefited from the use of prefabricated wood as a building material.

La construction de cette maison met à profit l'expérience très positive faite avec le bois préfabriqué.

Beim Bau dieses Hauses wurde auf die sehr guten Erfahrungen mit vorfabriziertem Holzbau zurückgegriffen.

The windows, set from floor level between the solar-paneled walls, contribute to the brightness and openness of the interior. The use of pale wood adds the perfect to

Les fenêtres allant jusqu'à l'étage et installées entre les murs solaires, font de l'intérieur un espace clair et ouvert. Le bois clair exalte cette impression.

Die geschosshohen Südfenster zwischen den Solarwänden lassen den Innenraum hell und offen erscheinen. Das helle Holz verstärkt diesen Eindruck.

☐ Wintergartenhaus

Robert Laur

This project is part of a series of standard houses based on the passive-house concept and using a specific construction system for houses made of timber. With a structure of wooden frames, the main feature of this modified system is the interior insulating layer which serves as an installation zone for cables and forms a structure of solid-wood supporting beams. OSB panels (oriented strand board) are attached to the outside of the solid-wood frame, combining to create a strong protected and completely airtight zone. The assembling process resembles that of a platform and offers definite advantages, such as easy low-cost connections and high-quality prefabrication for quick assembly. The substantial amount of solar energy collected thanks to the extensive glass surface supplies all of passive energy required by this type of house. It provides great lighting and spaciousness, as well as smaller, more intimate spaces.

Ce projet fait partie d'une série de maisons-types, construites selon la technique des maisons passives, utilisant un système particulier de construction en bois. Ce système est une variante des constructions à armature bois et a pour propriété de présenter une couche d'isolation intérieure servant aussi de zone d'installation de câbles, formant un système de poutres porteuses en bois massif. Sur l'extérieur de ce cadre, sont accrochés des panneaux OSB (oriented strand board), constituant une zone protégée et solide parfaitement hermétique à l'air. Le procédé de montage ressemble à celui d'une plate-forme avec les avantages de raccordements faciles, peu coûteux et d'une excellente qualité de préfabrication, garantissant un montage rapide. L'importante quantité d'énergie solaire obtenue par l'étendue de la surface vitrée, assure l'utilisation d'énergie passive de ce type de bâtiment. Cette maison, en dépit de l'impression de clarté et de transparence donnée, offre suffisamment d'espaces où l'intimité est preservée.

Dieses Projekt gehört zu einer Reihe von Typenhäusern in Passivhausbauweise, bei denen ein spezielles Holzbausystem angewendet wurde. Das System ist eine Abwandlung des Holzrahmenbaus und ist dadurch gekennzeichnet, dass die innere Dämmebene, die gleichzeitig als Installationsebene dient, durch das tragende Vollholzständerwerk gebildet wird. Auf der Aussenseite des Vollholzrahmens sind OSB-Platten (oriented strand board) befestigt, die gleichzeitig eine gut geschützte und robuste Luftdichtungsebene bilden. Der Montageablauf entspricht dem einer Plattformbauweise mit den Vorteilen einfacher, kostengünstiger Verbindungen und einem hohen Vorfertigungsgrad, der einen schnellen Aufbau garantiert. Die große Menge an Solarenergie, die durch die verglasten Bereiche gewonnen wird, garantiert die passivhausgerechte Nutzung dieses Haustypes. Trotz des hellen und offenen Gesamteindruckes den dieses Haus vermittelt, gibt es Rückzugsbereiche, die ausreichend Intimität gewährleisten.

great amount of solar energy collected thanks to the large bay window meets all the energy requirements of this type of passive house.

rande quantité d'énergie solaire, obtenue grâce à l'importante surface vitrée, assure les besoins énergétiques de ce type de maison passive.

große Menge an Solarenergie, die durch die verglasten Bereiche gewonnen wird, garantiert die passivhausgerechte Nutzung dieses Haustypes.

House on the island of Omø
Maison sur l'île d'Omø
Haus auf der Insel Omø

Ole Holst

In this project, the relationship between an elemental volume in cubic form and a construction based on the traditional techniques of the region creates an architectural language that is simple but compositionally strong. A determining requirement in the construction was the thermal insulation that, in this case, allows great energy savings. The fifteen centimeter thick floors and walls and the roofs of twenty centimeters guarantee great insulation, such that during winter heat is only used at the lowest levels. For cooling, the horizontal orientation of projecting wood battens on the exterior cladding reduce the exposure to direct sun up to 40% during the hottest months. This house shows, through an elemental layout in which it mainly uses indigenous materials, how an ecological, sustainable, and singular building can be created.

Dans ce projet, la relation entre un volume élémentaire de forme cubique et une construction basée sur les techniques traditionnelles de la région crée un langage architectural simple mais fort sur le plan de la composition. Le facteur déterminant de la construction est l'isolation thermique, qui, dans ce cas, permet de réduire considérablement la consommation d'énergie. Les sols et les murs d'une épaisseur de 15 centimètres et les plafonds de 20 garantissent une excellente isolation, qui permet en hiver d'utiliser le chauffage à un niveau minimum. Par ailleurs, la disposition horizontale des planches de bois de l'habillage extérieur contrôle jusqu'à quarante pour cent de l'incidence des rayons solaires durant les mois les plus chauds. Cette maison prouve qu'il est possible de réaliser une construction écologique, durable et originale, à partir d'un schéma élémentaire et des mêmes matériaux de construction que ceux utilisés dans la région.

Bei der Planung dieses Hauses entstand durch die Beziehung zwischen dem grundlegenden, würfelförmigen Körper und einer Bauweise, die auf den traditionellen, regionalen Techniken basiert, eine architektonische Ausdrucksweise, die einfach ist, aber eine große, zusammenfügende Kraft besitzt. Besonders wichtig war dabei die thermische Isolierung, durch die viel Energie gespart wird. Die Böden, die fünfzehn Zentimeter dicken Wände und das zwanzig Zentimeter dicke Dach isolieren das Haus sehr gut, so dass man im Winter nur minimal heizen muss. Durch die horizontale Anordnung der Holzbretter an der Außenverkleidung kann man das Einfallen der Sonnenstrahlen in den heißen Monaten um vierzig Prozent verringern. Dieses Haus ist ein Beweis dafür, wie man mit einem einfachen System, für das hauptsächlich die in der Region üblichen Materialien verwendet wurden, ein ökologisches, nachhaltiges und einzigartiges Haus schaffen kann.

Site plan Plan de situation Umgebungsplan

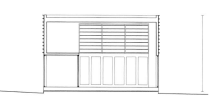

West elevation Élévation ouest Westlicher Aufriss

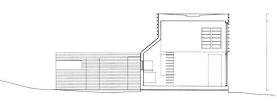

Cross section Section transversale Querschnitt

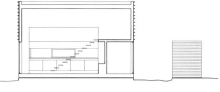

Longitudinal section Section longitudinale Längsschnitt

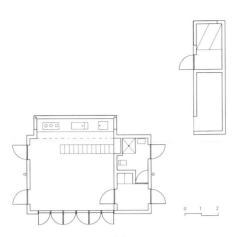

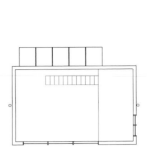

Ground floor Rez-de-chaussée Erdgeschoss

First floor Premier étage Erstes Obergeschoss

raised level provides the space for a bed, a bathroom and a spacious wardrobe.

niveau surélevé accueille le lit, la salle de bains et un placard très spacieux.

e Ebene, auf der sich das Bett befindet, ist erhöht und beherbergt zugleich das Badezimmer und einen großräumigen Wandschrank.

Parkstraße House
Maison de la Parkstraße
Haus Parkstraße

Rongen Architekten

This project involved the construction of a house made up of three apartments of different sizes on a narrow strip of land. Emphasis was given to the main body of the house with a clear structure and optimum use of the space available. The main body consists of two distinct sections: one clad in black tile with a flat roof, and the other wood-sided with a shed roof. The two bodies forming the building are built of cellular concrete and give a solid appearance. The architects had to follow strict ecological considerations for the whole ensemble, such as the use of non-polluting materials and an efficient energy system. Untreated larch wood was used exclusively for the wood façade and the terrace flooring – including the roof terrace. As the principal objective was energy-efficiency, the main living spaces were designed essentially to enjoy the sunlight and make full use of its heat, while secondary rooms were made to face north.

Le projet était de construire, sur un terrain très étroit, une maison dotée de trois appartements de tailles différentes. Dans ce projet, l'accent est mis sur un corps de bâtiment clairement structuré et sur l'optimalisation de l'espace disponible. Le corps de bâtiment est constitué de deux sections : une avec un toit plat recouvert de tuiles noires et une partie habillée de bois, coiffée d'un toit à un versant. Les deux corps de bâtiment sont massifs et construits en béton cellulaire. L'ensemble a été réalisé selon des considérations foncièrement écologiques. Les architectes ne devaient donc utiliser aucun matériau polluant et envisager un système d'énergie efficace. La façade en bois et le revêtement de toutes les terrasses – y compris la terrasse de toit – ont été réalisés exclusivement en bois de mélèze non traité. L'objectif étant de garantir l'efficacité énergétique, les espaces de vie sont essentiellement orientés vers le soleil pour alimenter l'énergie solaire, les pièces secondaires étant orientées vers le nord.

Auf einem sehr schmalen Grundstück sollte ein Haus mit drei unterschiedlich großen Wohnungen entstehen. Der Schwerpunkt des Entwurfs lag in einer klaren Baukörperstruktur und der größtmöglichen Ausnutzung des zur Verfügung stehenden Raumes. Der Baukörper besteht aus zwei Segmenten: ein mit schwarzem Klinker verblendeter Flachdachteil sowie ein holzverkleideter Teil mit Pultdach. Beide Baukörper sind massiv aus Porenbeton gemauert. Das gesamte Gebäude wurde nach streng ökologischen Gesichtspunkten errichtet, dass hieß für den Architekten, keine schädlichen Baustoffe zu verarbeiten und auf Energieeffizienz zu achten. So wurde für die Holzfassade und den Bodenbelag aller Terrassen – einschließlich der Dachterrassen – nur unbehandeltes Lärchenholz verwendet. Um die Energieeffizienz zu gewährleisten, orientieren sich die Aufenthaltsräume ausschließlich zur Sonnenseite um so solare Energie zu gewinnen; die untergeordneten Räume dagegen sind nach Norden hin ausgerichtet.

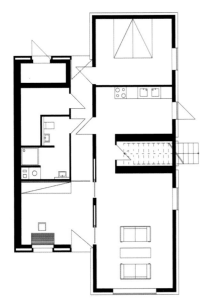

Ground floor Rez-de-chaussée Erdgeschoss

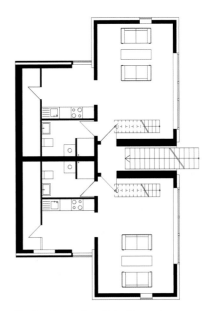

First floor Premier étage Erstes Obergeschoss

ear architectural structure and optimum use of the space available have been the most important elements of this project.

s ce projet, l'accent est mis sur une structure architecturale claire et une optimisation de l'espace disponible.

Schwerpunkt beim Entwurf dieses Projektes lag in einer klaren Baukörperstruktur und der größtmöglichen Ausnutzung des zur Verfügung stehenden Raumes.

Untreated larch wood is the only material used for the wood façade and the flooring of all the terraces.

Le bois de mélèze non traité est l'unique matériau employé pour l'habillage de la façade et le revêtement de toutes les terrasses.

Als Konstruktionsmaterial wurde sowohl für die Holzfassade als auch für den Bodenbelag aller Terrassen ausschließlich unbehandeltes Lärchenholz verwendet.

☐ Riera House

Maison Riera

Riera Haus

Estudio BC Architects

This project was the first work of the architects to fully realize their ideas of bioclimatic architecture and it has brought them several important commissions. The challenge was to create a house that exploits the natural insulating and cooling properties of earth-sheltered construction, but at the same time feels comfortable and open. Both counts were achieved by taking advantage of the thermal mass of the ground, which keeps the interior cool in summer, and the double-glazed windows, which can be shaded from direct sun by horizontal shutters and a canvas awning that extends over the living room terrace. All windows and doors can be opened for natural ventilation, drawing in cool breezes off the sea. In winter the shutters are raised during the day and lowered at night, allowing the floor to absorb and retain the heat of the low sun. This passive solar gain is supplemented by electric ceiling heating that costs only a third of what it would be in a conventional house.

Ce projet est la première œuvre des architectes dans laquelle ils réalisent totalement leurs idées d'architecture bioclimatique, leur valant diverses commandes importantes. L'enjeu était de créer une maison qui exploite l'isolation naturelle et les propriétés de refroidissement naturel, tout en restant confortable et ouverte. Les deux objectifs ont été atteints en tirant profit à la fois de la masse thermique du sol, qui, en été, maintient la fraîcheur à l'intérieur et des fenêtres à double vitrage protégées du soleil direct par des volets horizontaux et des vélums en toile qui s'étendent au-dessus de la terrasse du salon. Toutes les fenêtres et portes sont disposées de façon à créer une ventilation naturelle, profitant de la fraîcheur des brises marines. En hivers, les volets pensent être réglés pour permettre au sol d'absorber et de retenir la chaleur des faibles rayons du soleil. Cette énergie solaire passive est complétée par un chauffage de plafond électrique, générant ainsi un tiers du coût de celui d'une maison conventionnelle.

Bei diesem Bauprojekt konnten die Architekten zum ersten Mal ihre Ideen zur bioklimatischen Bauweise vollständig umsetzen und es verhalf ihnen zu verschiedenen, wichtigen Aufträgen. Die Planer stellten sich der Herausforderung, ein Haus zu schaffen, das die natürliche Isolierung und Kühlung nutzt, aber gleichzeitig komfortabel und offen ist. Beide Ziele erreichte man, indem man die thermale Masse des Bodens ausnutzte, um das Innere im Sommer zu kühlen, und durch Doppelglasfenster, die mit Fensterläden und Planen, die auch die Wohnterrasse überdachen, vor der direkten Sonneneinstrahlung geschützt werden. Alle Fenster und Türen sind auf eine Art und Weise angeordnet, um auf natürlichem Wege zu lüften und die kühle Seeluft ins Haus zu lassen. Im Winter können die Fensterläden so reguliert werden, dass der Fußboden die Wärme der niedrigen Sonne aufnehmen und speichern kann. Dieser passive Wärmegewinn aus der Sonne wird durch eine elektrische Heizung ergänzt, die aber nur ein Drittel der Kosten eines konventionellen Hauses verursacht.

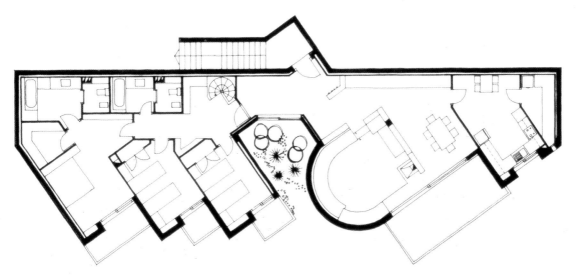

Plan Plan Grundriss

Regarded as a true living architectural creation, this house owes a considerable part of its charm to the growing vegetation around it.

Le charme de cette maison, considérée comme une création architecturale vivante, ne fait que croître au rythme de la verdure grandissante.

Das Haus kann als lebende architektonische Schöpfung betrachtet werden und gewinnt mit zunehmender Begrünung immer mehr an Charme.

Livingscape

Graeme North Architects

As a prominent earth building practitioner, the architect designed this project as his own livingspace and at the same time as a site to conduct workshops and demonstrations in earth building for tertiary students. Besides the particular interest in the integrated relationship between plants and buildings, his aim was to apply alternative technologies such as recycling or reusing of various materials like the old fire bricks and bottles set in lime mortar, used for the wall construction. Also low energy and low cost building methods were fundamental, as was the installation of a solar hot water heater with a wood fire backup. Plants intertwine throughout the whole space so that the boundaries between inside and outside are very blurred. While the plants are chosen partially for their productivity (eg grapes, kiwi fruit) they also act as shading mechanisms during summer, evaporative coolers, and air filtres.

Eminent praticien de la construction de terre, l'architecte a conçu ce projet pour son propre espace de vie. Il y organise aussi des ateliers et des démonstrations sur le thème de l'architecture de terre destinés aux étudiants du troisième cycle. En dehors de l'intérêt particulier que présente la relation étroite entre plantes et constructions, son objectif est d'utiliser des technologies alternatives comme le recyclage ou le réemploi de divers matériaux, à l'instar de vieilles briques et bouteilles mélangées à un mortier à la chaux, utilisé pour la construction de murs. Les méthodes de consommation d'énergie réduite et de construction à faibles coûts sont ici également fondamentales, comme l'installation d'un chauffe-eau à énergie solaire complété par un chauffage à bois d'appoint. L'espace est rempli de plantes entrelacées, effaçant les limites entre l'intérieur et l'extérieur. Sélectionnées en partie pour leur productivité (raisins, kiwi), elles jouent, en été, également le rôle de générateur d'ombre, de climatiseurs et de filtres à air.

Der Architekt, ein bekannter Fachmann für die Erdbauweise, entwarf dieses Haus für sich selbst. Er veranstaltet hier auch Workshops und Vorführungen für Studenten zum Thema Erdbauweise. Ein besonderes Interesse des Architekten war es, eine integrierte Beziehung zwischen den Pflanzen und dem Gebäude zu schaffen, und außerdem alternative Technologien wie Recycling und Wiederverwendung verschiedener Materialien anzuwenden. So benutzte er beispielsweise alte Brandziegel und Flaschen in Kalkmörtel für die Konstruktion der Wände. Ebenso wichtig waren ihm die energie- und kostensparende Bauweise, deshalb wurden Sonnenkollektoren für das Warmwasser mit einem zusätzlichen, mit Holz betriebenem Heizsystem installiert. Pflanzen winden sich über das gesamte Gebäude, so dass die Grenzen zwischen innen und außen verschwimmen. Sie wurden aufgrund ihrer Produktivität ausgewählt, so gibt es beispielweise Trauben und Kiwis. Im Sommer spenden sie Schatten, kühlen das Haus und filtern die Luft.

king the outdoor greenery part of the architecture is the key element in the design of this house, occupied by the architect himself.

tégration de la végétation environnante à l'architecture est l'idée phare de l'architecte, habitant lui-même la maison.

Integration der umgebenden Pflanzenwelt in die Architektur ist eine der Hauptvisionen des Architekten und zugleich Bewohner des Hauses.

Recycled objects, such as glass bottles used as interior decoration elements, play an important part in this project.

Le recyclage d'objets joue un rôle essentiel dans ce projet, à l'instar de bouteilles de verre utilisées comme éléments de décoration intérieure.

Das Recycling von Objekten spielt bei diesem Projekt eine wichtige Rolle und so wurden beispielsweise Glasflaschen als Dekorationselemente wiederverwertet.

☐ Villa Långbo

Olavi Koponen

With a simple structure and areas that are individually defined based on lighting, this building has been constructed with the aspiration of removing the barrier between the building and its surroundings. Located on the extreme west-side of the island and exposed to the prevailing winds, the house is situated on the edge of the forest which allows it to see be partially seen from the sea while its occupants may gaze upon the same sea from any of the rooms. At the mercy of the conditions of a freezing and thawing sea, the house is only accessible by boat or on skis, rendering it unusable at certain times of the year. All the materials are recyclable. The wood is locally harvested, the construction done by hand, and the materials transported by horse during the winter. All this was done in order to make sure that the environment was disturbed as little as possible.

Doté d'une structure simple et d'espaces de vie définis indivi-
duellement en fonction de la lumière naturelle, cet édifice est
construit pour se fondre dans l'environnement. Implantée à
l'extrémité est de l'île et exposée aux vents, la maison se situe
en bordure de la forêt. Vue partiellement depuis la mer, ses
habitants, en revanche, ont une vue panoramique sur les flots
depuis n'importe qu'elle pièce. L'accès à ce bâtiment, dans
une région soumise au gel et dégel de la mer, n'est pas toujours possible. Il n'est possible de s'y rendre qu'en bateau,
parfois en ski. Il n'est donc pas utilisable toute l'année. Tous
les matériaux sont recyclables et le bois utilisé vient de la
région même. La construction est réalisée de manière artisa-
nale et les matériaux sont transportés à cheval pendant l'hiver. Tout a été mis en œuvre pour minimiser l'impact de la
construction sur l'environnement.

Dieses Haus mit seiner einfachen Struktur und den individuell
durch die Art der Beleuchtung definierten Bereiche wurde mit
der Absicht gebaut, die Barriere zwischen dem Gebäude und der
Umgebung aufzulösen. Das Haus befindet sich im Westen der
Insel und ist den vorherrschenden Winden ausgesetzt. Es liegt
direkt neben einem Wald und man sieht nur Teile des Hauses
vom Meer aus, während man vom Inneren das Meer von allen
Räumen aus ungehindert sehen kann. Da das Meer in dieser
Gegend friert und wieder taut, ist das Gebäude nicht immer
zugänglich. Manchmal erreicht man es nur im Boot, manchmal
nur auf Skiern, es ist also nicht das ganze Jahr über bewohnbar.
Alle Materialien können recycelt werden. Das verwendete Holz
stammt aus der gleichen Region, das Haus wurde in Handarbeit
errichtet und die Materialien wurden im Winter mit Pferden
transportiert. All diese Anstrengungen unternahm man, um die
Umwelt so wenig wie möglich zu verändern.

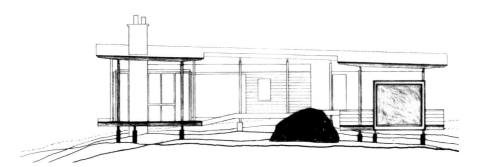

Elevation Élévation Aufriss

☐ Hasenhof

Sturm & Wartzeck

Hasenhof stands on farmland that is still worked today. A 1930s house with a timber frame was built here but had to be razed to its foundations as it was threatening to collapse. Only the sandstone base of the small original house remained and served as the base for the erection of this new building. The characteristics of the exterior are typical of the vernacular architecture of the Rhein Valley, while the interiors are distinctically modern and spacious. The untreated larch wood used to build the main structure is a fine example of the renewable building materials used exclusively for the construction and extension of this building. Due to the careful and sophisticated use of thermal insulation and vapor barriers, the water and space heating fuel requirements were cut down to only 600 liters per year. This, as well as the type of fuel used, also reduces costs.

Le Hasenhof fait partie d'un corps de ferme installé hors du village et encore exploité actuellement. L'ancienne maison à colombages, implantée autrefois sur ce terrain, datait des années trente. Délabrée, elle a été entièrement démolie, hormis les fondations. Ensuite, la nouvelle construction a été installée sur le socle de grés de l'ancienne petite ferme. L'apparence extérieure du corps de bâtiment est déterminée par l'architecture traditionnelle de la Rhön, alors que l'espace intérieur affiche un plan ouvert et moderne. Construction et restauration ont été effectuées en employant strictement et exclusivement des matériaux écologiques. A titre d'exemple, l'isolation phonique extérieure est entièrement réalisée à base de mélèze non traité. Une parfaite et judicieuse isolation phonique et thermique permet de réduire les besoins énergétiques au minimum. Convertis en frais de mazout, pour l'eau chaude et le chauffage, ils ne représentent que 600 litres à l'année.

Der Hasenhof gehört zu einem gewachsenen Aussiedlergehöft, das noch heute bewirtschaftet wird. Das einst auf dem Grundstück gelegene Fachwerkhaus stammte noch aus den 30er Jahren und wurde wegen Baufälligkeit bis auf die Grundmauern abgerissen. Daraufhin wurde der Neubau auf dem Sandsteinsockel des ehemaligen Austragshäuschens errichtet. Bestimmend für das äußere Erscheinungsbild des Baukörpers ist die traditionelle bäuerliche Architektur der Rhön, während der Innenraum von einem modernen, offenen Grundriss gekennzeichnet ist. Beim Bau und Ausbau wurde streng auf die Verwendung ausschließlich ökologischer Baustoffe geachtet, so wurde beispielsweise die komplette Außenschalung mit unbehandelter Lärche gemacht. Durch ein sorgfältig ausgearbeitetes Dämmungs- und Isolierungssystem ist der Energiebedarf auf ein Minimum reduziert und beträgt für Wasser- und Heizungskosten auf Heizöl umgerechnet im Jahr nur 600 Liter.

asenhof is located just outside the village, on farmland that is still worked today.

e Hasenhof fait partie d'un corps de ferme installé hors du village, encore exploité actuellement.

er Hasenhof gehört zu einem gewachsenen Aussiedlergehöft aus den 30er Jahren, das noch heute bewirtschaftet wird.

The new building has been erected on the sandstone base of the old house, originally leased out to the farmer and his family. The external appearance of its main body a typical example of traditional farm architecture.

La nouvelle construction a été installée sur le socle de grés de l'ancienne petite maison donnée au fermier dans le cadre du bail familial. L'apparence extérieure du co de bâtiment affiche une architecture paysanne traditionnelle.

Der Neubau wurde auf dem Sockel des ehemaligen Austragshäuschens errichtet und sein Erscheinungsbild ist von einer traditionellen bäuerlichen Architektur geprägt

The interior has an open, modern layout which allows sufficient daylight to come in.

L'espace intérieur suit un plan ouvert et moderne, assurant partout une incidence suffisante de la lumière.

Der Innenraum ist von einem modernen, offenen Grundriss gekennzeichnet, der ausreichend Lichteinfall aus unterschiedlichen Richtungen garantiert.

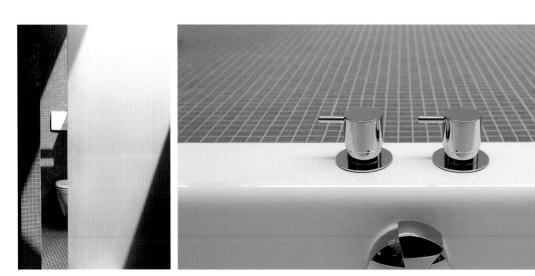

☐ Villa Hengeveld

J. P. Moehrlein, MAD Moehrleinvandelft

In 2001, the Haren Council launched the ambitious De Mikkelhorst model-project initiative, based on the sustainable construction concept. Making efficient use of space, this project consists of eight houses designed and built following the so-called 'sustainable-building dimensions' and other features of bioclimatic construction methods. The long and narrow site, used for the eight-house complex and on which Villa Hengeveld stands, is divided by walls separating public and private spaces. The building was designed to take full advantage of the orientation of the sun, with the garden and the terraced roofs – accessible from the bedrooms through sliding glass doors – facing the sunniest side. A heat accumulator and photovoltaic panels work together with the combined-cycle gas heater to provide both heating and hot water for general domestic use.

En 2001, la commune de Haren pris l'initiative de créer le projet modèle De Mikkelhorst, concrétisant ainsi ses grandes ambitions sur le plan de la construction durable. Cette réalisation comprend 8 maisons où sont appliquées les dispositions de ce mode de construction alternatif sur divers plans : conception, mode de construction et exploitation de l'espace habitable. La parcelle étroite et tout en longueur, accueillant les huit habitations, dont la Villa Hengeveld, a été subdivisée en zones « à usage publique » et sphères privées par le biais de panneaux et de cloisons. L'édifice « s'ouvre » selon un plan méthodique vers les cotés exposés aux intempéries : les jardins et les terrasses de toit sont accessibles depuis les espaces de vies par de grandes parois coulissantes tout en hauteur. La chaudière mixte à gaz utilisée pour le chauffage est équipée d'un accumulateur et de capteurs solaires. De même, le système de chauffage d'eaux à usage domestique peut être alimenté à la chaleur solaire.

Die Gemeinde Haren ergriff im Jahre 2001 die Initiative, ihren hohen Ehrgeiz hinsichtlich des nachhaltigen Bauens (NaBa) in dem Modellprojekt De Mikkelhorst umzusetzen. Das Projekt umfasst 8 Wohnhäuser, bei denen die so genannten NaBa-Maßnahmen sowohl im Entwurf, als auch bezüglich der Bauweise und Wohnungsnutzung berücksichtigt wurden. Die lange, schmale Parzelle, auf der die Hengeveld-Villa als eines der acht Wohnhäuser steht, wurde mittels gemauerter Wandscheiben zwischen der „öffentlichen Praxis-Funktion" und dem privaten Bereich unterteilt. Das Gebäude öffnet sich programmatisch zu den Wetterseiten, indem die Gärten und Dachterrassen durch große, geschosshohe Schiebefronten von den Wohnräumen aus erreichbar sind. Der zum Heizen verwendete Gas-Kombikessel ist mit Solarspeicher und Sonnenkollektoren ausgestattet, sowie die Brauchwasseranlage, die solarthermisch betrieben wird.

front of the house opens directly onto a spacious terrace, with both shade and sunlight for those wishing to sit outside.

ant la maison, une terrasse spacieuse, directement reliée à l'espace intérieur, permet de s'asseoir à l'ombre ou au soleil.

dem Haus befindet sich eine geräumige Terrasse, die direkt mit dem Innenraum verbunden ist und sowohl im Schatten als auch in der Sonne Sitzgelegenheiten bietet.

The unique shape of the house catches the eye from a distance, while blending perfectly with the landscape.

La forme originale de la maison attire l'attention de loin, tout en s'insérant harmonieusement au coeur du paysage.

Die außergewöhnliche Form des Hauses erregt selbst aus der Ferne Aufmerksamkeit, fügt sich jedoch harmonisch in das Landschaftsbild ein.

Photo credits Crédits photographiques Fotonachweis

p. 12-19   JD Peterson

p. 20-29   Grazia Ike-Branco

p. 30-37   Herman van Doorn

p. 38-43   Rongen Architekten

p. 44-51   Rongen Architekten

p. 52-59   Rongen Architekten

p. 60-67   Architekturbüro Rolf Disch

p. 68-75   Miguel de Guzmán

p. 76-83   Arnoud Kos Fotografie

p. 84-93   Bruno Klomfar, James Morris

p. 94-103   Helene Grégoire

p. 104-111   Claudio Santini, JD Peterson

p. 112-119   Janet Delaney

p. 120-127   Frédérik Comptesse

p. 128-133   Johannes Marburg

p. 134-139   Ole Holst

p. 140-149   Rongen Architekten

p. 150-155   Luis Casals

p. 156-161   Graeme North Architects

p. 162-171   Jussi Tianien

p. 172-181   Johannes Marburg

p. 182-189   SAPh, Rob de Jong